Original title:
In the Shadow of Cedars

Copyright © 2025 Creative Arts Management OÜ
All rights reserved.

Author: Rory Fitzgerald
ISBN HARDBACK: 978-1-80567-368-2
ISBN PAPERBACK: 978-1-80567-667-6

Beneath the Gnarled Branches

Squirrels dance in nutty glee,
While birds gossip high on a tree.
A raccoon steals a picnic snack,
He slips away, no need to act.

Beneath the twisted limbs so wide,
A rabbit hops, and tries to hide.
But with a thump, he trips and falls,
The forest echoes with his calls.

Nature's Sanctuary of Serenity

A frog croaks out a silly tune,
While ants march by, in grand festoon.
The buzzing bees forgot their route,
And one gets stuck in Bear's snoot!

The breezy leaves begin to sway,
Whispering secrets of the day.
A deer prances, but trips on grass,
Now it's looking thoroughly crass.

Lost Dogma of the Green

A turtle thinks he's on the run,
But really moves at snail-like fun.
While bunnies plot to steal his shell,
But who could blame them? It's quite swell!

The flowers giggle as they bloom,
At all the critters' clumsy zoom.
A hedgehog tries to join the race,
But trips on roots—it's not his place.

The Wisdom of Woodland Shadows

An owl gives life advice at night,
"Don't be the mouse—don't pick a fight."
While fireflies interrupt his class,
"Excuse us, but must flash and pass!"

The shadows play tricks on the eyes,
Making owls look like funny spies.
As the sun sets, they begin to prance,
Those woodland creatures seize their chance.

Raindrops' Melody on Cedar

Raindrops tap, a playful beat,
Squirrels dance, with tiny feet.
Puddles form, then splash away,
As frogs croak out the rainy play.

Trees wear crowns of glistening dew,
Each leaf a hat, in nature's hue.
A groundhog grins, peeks from his den,
Singing to the rhythm of the glen.

An Ode to the Sylvan Heart

A beaver builds, with lumber flair,
While owls hoot, suspending air.
The tallest tree, it sways and creaks,
Whispering secrets, as nature speaks.

Chipmunks race on sunlight's edge,
Gathering nuts near a mossy ledge.
With every twist, a comic fall,
Nature laughs, inviting all.

The Forest's Endless Embrace

Branches bounce in a breezy jig,
While rabbits hop, oh so big!
Beneath the boughs, a picnic spread,
With sandwiches made, on a cozy bed.

A fox trots by, in a sneaky stroll,
Looking for snacks, that's his goal.
Chipmunks taunt, with every bite,
In this woodland, life's pure delight.

Paths Worn by Time and Tree

Footprints tread on a winding road,
Chasing stories, laying a load.
Old roots speak of days gone by,
While wise old branches reach for the sky.

Laughter echoes among the trees,
As friends gather, making their pleas.
With tales of mischief, they share and boast,
In this woodland, they love the most.

Hues of Nature's Embrace

Leaves are laughing, swaying with glee,
The sun's a jester, dancing free.
Lizards doing their little jig,
While squirrels throw acorns, it's quite big!

A deer slips on a grassy patch,
With a thud, a funny match!
Painted skies, a comic scene,
Nature's circus, vibrant and keen.

In the Arms of Old Growth

Mossy giants, ancient and sly,
Whisper secrets as birds fly by.
Beneath the branches, critters collide,
A raccoon in a hat, oh what a ride!

The woodpecker's tap is a concert grand,
While chipmunks chime in, lend a hand.
Nature's chuckle, rich and bright,
Old growth musings, pure delight.

Twilight Among the Trunks

Evening settles, shadows play,
With fireflies lighting the way.
Owls hoot jokes that tickle the ear,
While the moon giggles, less than clear.

Bats swoop down, a game of tag,
Laughter echoes, a twilight brag.
Crickets chirp in a rhythmic tune,
Nature's comedy beneath the moon.

Enchanted by Evergreen Sighs

Pine needles rustle, secrets expressed,
Frogs join in, their voices impressed.
A squirrel slips, then strikes a pose,
As laughter bubbles from nearby crows.

Jays cackle at their own little games,
While trees watch on, whispering names.
Nature's laughter, soothing and wide,
In this green realm, joy cannot hide.

The Ancestral Echoes of Trees

In the forest where whispers play,
Old trees gossip night and day.
Their branches sway with juicy tales,
Of squirrels' pranks and windy gales.

A chipmunk's dance, a raccoon's flight,
These are the stories brought to light.
With roots like gossip, deep and wide,
The trees share secrets, side by side.

Stories Written in the Bark

In grooves and lines, the tales unfold,
Of summer suns and winters cold.
Each scratch a giggle, each knot a grin,
They tell of journeys that begin.

Some claim the trees have seen it all,
From lovebirds' calls to squirrels' brawl.
So next time you pass by a tree,
Just pause and listen, you might agree!

Hiding Places of the Heart

Within thick trunks, the secrets sit,
A hidden love that once was lit.
A bark carved heart with dates and names,
Of silly lovers' silly games.

Behind the boughs, a wink, a peek,
Where shy hearts dart and cheek to cheek.
The laughter rings like summer's glee,
In spots where no one else can see.

Emblems of Earth's Resilience

Amongst the storms that bark and bite,
There stands a tree, a comical sight.
With leaves that dance like jester's hats,
It sways and bends, like playful cats.

Each ring a laugh at passing years,
While roots hold tight despite the fears.
Oh, nature's jesters stand so bold,
Emblems of life, a tale retold.

Veil of Needles and Time

The trees wear caps of green,
Like grandmas at a party scene.
Branches scratch like tiny claws,
While squirrels munch without a pause.

One shouted, "Hey! I'm a tree!"
Another winked, "Just let me be!"
Rabbits giggle, foxes play,
Nature's circus, come what may.

With pine cones raining down like stars,
And deer who've crashed the car from Mars,
The forest laughs in the bright sun's crumb,
'Cause who would think trees could be so dumb?

So next time you hear a rustle near,
Just know it's laughter, not a fear.
Among the boughs, pranks come to bloom,
In this green world, we all make room.

Wandering Through Whispering Woods

I wandered through the leafy maze,
Where trees play tricks and squirrels gaze.
They wink and nod with secret jokes,
As if they're sly, wise tree-folk folks.

A raccoon asked, "Would you believe,
These branches hide a real-life thief?"
A squirrel squeaked, "He stole my nut,
Banana peels? Misplaced a cut!"

Each trunk was like a talking friend,
With barky tales that never end.
The path would tease with roots that trip,
And moss that sneaks to steal a sip.

But in the laughter of the leaves,
You'd miss the fact that all trees grieve.
For when the sun begins to set,
They pine for company, I bet!

Beneath the Spires of Green

Beneath the tall ones, quite serene,
I met a gopher, rather keen.
He danced around in muddy shoes,
And asked if I would share his views.

"Why rush?" he said, with dirt on his face,
In these woods, there's plenty of space.
We'll hop like frogs and spin like tops,
And shed our woes, they're just like flops."

A woodpecker drummed a funny beat,
While dancing ants moved on their feet.
Each blade of grass a whispering bark,
Echoed the laughter, lit up the dark.

So if you find a place like this,
With trees that sway and nature's bliss,
Join the party, don't hesitate,
For every night's a funny fate!

The Silence of Tall Sentinels

Those towering trees, they stand so still,
Guarding secrets, yet they thrill.
Their shadows dance upon the ground,
As if they're sharing something profound.

But wait! What's that? A shaky sound,
A bear in glasses, round and round!
He's reading books, quite out of style,
And asks, "Do I look cute? Do I make you smile?"

The owls nearby hoot in delight,
They both conspire to fuel the night.
Around them dance the vines and ferns,
In laughter's grip, the forest turns.

With strobes of moonlight on their way,
The trees can't help but feel the play.
For underneath the silent sheen,
They love the noise of all unseen!

A Celebration of Green Vistas

In the forest so bright, we frolic and play,
The leaves overhead dance, come join the ballet.
Squirrels plot in the trees, with acorns in tow,
While rabbits chuckle loud, in the grass they do grow.

Tripping over roots, with laughter we meet,
A picnic spreads wide, as ants find our treat.
In the shade, we can nap, beneath boughs' embrace,
Then wake to a breeze with a grin on our face.

The Breath of Silent Sentinels

Tall trunks stand proud, with a stellar façade,
They whisper and creak, our own forest band.
A woodpecker knocks, like a drummer's own beat,
As chipmunks do scurry, trying not to cheat.

Bees buzz in a hurry, no time for a chat,
While owls share jokes that are not where it's at.
The raccoons are plotting their next daring heist,
For snacks from our lunch, oh, how they are enticed!

Constellations of Leaves Above

Look up and behold, the leafy delights,
Each branch tells a story, from days and nights.
Twinkling green stars, in a milky blue sea,
We ponder their travels, just you and me.

With branches so thick, it's a leafy parade,
Guessing the patterns, we laugh and we trade.
A toucan drops by, with a colorful shout,
As squirrels throw acorns, there's never a doubt!

Home Among the Swaying Giants

Wobble and sway, when the wind starts to play,
This leafy abode is where we'd like to stay.
With shadows that stretch, like a big friendly cat,
We dance in their sway, and giggle at that.

The toadstools all chuckle, they giggle so bright,
As critters debate if they're up for a fight.
In a home of tall giants, we share laughs anew,
And toast with our juice, under skies ever blue.

Echoes of the Forest Floor

Squirrels chatter, just a tease,
They're plotting snacks, if you please.
Mushrooms giggle as they sprout,
Twisting thoughts, without a doubt.

Leaves do dance, a silly waltz,
While shadows play their little faults.
Rabbits hop with jaunty flair,
And chipmunks strut without a care.

Frogs croak jokes beneath the trees,
While breezes carry playful glee.
In this realm where laughter blooms,
Nature's fun is free of gloom.

Beneath the Boughs

Under branches, secrets hide,
Where owls wink with gentle pride.
Bunnies bumble, tripping light,
In their race to catch some flight.

The sun, a jester, shines so bright,
While shadows play their tricks at night.
A raccoon wears a mask of fun,
Planning pranks until he's done.

Tickling vines, they twist and twine,
Engaging all in silly line.
Nature giggles, oh what a sight,
Beneath boughs, everything feels right.

Guardians of the Timbered Heights

Tall trees whisper tales of old,
About the antics they uphold.
Beetles march, a tiny band,
While moths plot mischief, oh so grand.

Bears lounge about, basking in sun,
They flip and flop, just having fun.
Raccoons sneak with crafty paws,
Their nightly escapades, full of flaws.

Every creature plays their role,
In this woodland circus, full of soul.
Guardians guard with winks and grins,
In timbered heights, the laughter spins.

Sylvan Reverie

In dreamlike woods, the giggles rise,
Where shadows dance in clever guise.
Grass tickles toes as one may tread,
Nature's laughter leads ahead.

Foxes prance, with tales to share,
The breeze chimes in, a gleeful air.
Whispers of leaves, a playful crowd,
Echoing laughter, laughter loud.

Moonlit nights bring playful sights,
Bats swoop low with silly flights.
In sylvan realms, where fun is free,
Join the frolic, come and see!

Fragments of Light Through Green Veils

Sunlight dances on green leaves,
A squirrel steals my sandwich, with ease.
Beams peek through like playful sprites,
Laughing at my picnic delights.

The breeze whispers secrets and sighs,
Tickles my nose, oh how time flies!
A bird overhead tries to sing,
Yet drops a twig—a comedic fling.

A beetle marches with great pride,
While ants form ranks and start to bide.
Nature's laugh echoes, a riotous tune,
As butterflies float like balloons in June.

The Embrace of Nature's Pillars

Beneath tall trunks, the shadows sprawl,
I trip on roots, oh how I fall!
With bark like sweaters, thick and warm,
Nature's embrace, a lumberjack charm.

Chirps and chuckles fill the air,
A frog croaks out a grand affair.
While vines swing low, like jesters cheer,
Tickling my toes, bringing me near.

I spy a raccoon, its mask on tight,
Searching my bag for a snack tonight.
In laughter we share this earthy space,
In the great outdoors, life's a race!

Musing Among the Majestic

Standing tall, oh mighty trees,
They sway and bow, like they're at ease.
A woodpecker taps a funny beat,
While I attempt to find my seat.

The squirrels hold a wild debate,
About acorns, their favorite fate.
I join in, pitching my own views,
But they scamper off, quick to choose.

Among the leaves, I ponder much,
Life's little quirks, that gentle touch.
Nature giggles, it knows the score,
Whispers of joy on this outdoor floor.

A Tapestry of Shade and Light

Dappled sunlight paints the ground,
A twirling leaf falls without a sound.
It lands right on my unsuspecting head,
Causing a chuckle—not much dread.

The wind gives chase to a wayward hat,
Like it's a game of nowhere to sat.
Through laughter and skip, I join the race,
In this playful, leafy embrace.

Nature's jokes, they never tire,
A sleeping bear, or a bird with lyre.
Among the trees, both grand and slight,
Life's a laugh in this woven light.

The Embrace of the Forest Floor

A squirrel drops acorns with grace,
They bounce and roll all over the place.
A chipmunk sighs, 'What a messy affair!'
While leaves wiggle, giggling in air.

Fungus grows quietly under the pine,
Whispering secrets of past and divine.
Worms throw a party right in the dirt,
While ants march home, covered in shirts.

The shadows hop, they dance and sway,
As butterflies flutter, the clowns of the day.
A deer trips over roots, oh what a sight,
With laughter echoing into the night.

Underneath Heaven's Tall Sentinels

Pinecones plop like the loudest of drums,
As owls hoot loudly, with glee, they come!
The sun peeks through, a flashlight on bees,
As squirrels yell, 'Hey, just look at these!'

Beneath the branches, the critters collide,
A family of raccoons go for a ride.
Chasing their tails in a hilarious run,
While the shadows creep in, and join in the fun.

A bird misfires its aim at a tree,
Lands on a branch, now it's lunch for a flea.
The forest chuckles with every little blunder,
As laughter rings out, warm like summer thunder.

The Memory of Rain on Wood

Raindrops plink like a drummer's beat,
They bounce on leaves, oh, what a treat!
A frog leaps high, thinking he's a king,
While puddles reflect all the silly things.

The toads croak out their own little tune,
As snails in their shells take the day off at noon.
Mushrooms pop up, wearing hats of gray,
In a fashion show that's hip in its way.

The taste of wet earth in a light-hearted kiss,
While a mouse tiptoes through puddles with bliss.
No storm can stop this joyful parade,
As laughter joins raindrops that never fade.

Shadows Cast by Silent Watchers

Trees lean in, like they're sharing a joke,
As winds play tag, set loose by a poke.
While shadows stretch out, a game of charades,
The creatures below are lost in escapades.

A woodpecker practices its stand-up set,
Knocking on bark, no sign of regret.
While chipmunks debate the best nut to claim,
Their little discussions, all part of the game.

The sun dips low, revealing mischief at play,
As fireflies blink, lighting up the display.
Nature's own theatre, with humor in tow,
In the stillness, giggles continue to grow.

Remnants of a Forgotten Path

Once I trod where creatures roamed,
Now just squirrels with acorn homes.
They roll their eyes at my slow pace,
As I trip over my shoelace!

Old footprints lost to time's embrace,
Chased by shadows, like a race.
They giggle softly, 'Look at him!'
Stumbling forward, laugh-filled whim!

Mossy signs mark where I missed,
A path that twists like a shopping list.
Oh! A detour where I can hop,
While nature giggles, won't let me stop!

But here I stand, crown of leaves worn,
With pinecone prizes unceremoniously borne.
The critters applaud my daring feat,
And I bow low, feeling quite neat.

The Dreamer's Refuge in Moss

In cozy corners where dreams nap,
A squirrel held court, adorned in a cap.
Telling tales of treasure on the hill,
But all I found was a paper mill!

Beneath the boughs, my ideas sprout,
Worried whispers, as I shout out.
An audience of insects, buzzing still,
They chuckle softly, fond of the thrill.

I pondered fate over mushrooms bright,
A banquet of fungi, quite a sight!
Yet, when I ventured to taste my find,
The critters erupted, 'You are so blind!'

With every sip of life's green tea,
I brewed confusion, oh woe is me!
Still, I laugh and weave my trippy tales,
In my sweet haven, where laughter prevails.

A Soliloquy of Needles and Leaves

Amidst the needles, I take a stand,
A piny throne, all unplanned.
With accents high, I start my show,
Pretending to be a leafy guru pro.

The leaves laugh softly, rustling with glee,
'What does he know? He's just tree debris!'
Yet I prance, arms waving wide,
While a crow caws, oh what a ride!

Pinecones drop like applause from the sky,
I somersault, oh, don't be shy!
The forest watches this spectacle grand,
Clapping with branches, oh isn't it grand?

But in my heart, I know the truth,
That comedy blooms not from quirk or sleuth.
Yet as I tumble and roll in mirth,
I claim my throne upon this earthy girth.

When the Wind Whispers Secrets

The wind curls in with gossip bold,
Tales of mischief from days of old.
It tickles my ears with every breeze,
Commanding respect from the shivering trees!

'Listen close!' it seems to say,
'Even leaves have dreams, in their own way.'
They flutter and flutter, what tales to weave,
Of a squirrel's heist, or the acorn thief!

Under canopies, giggles arise,
As branches sway like a dance with ties.
Whispering secrets of blunders past,
While I ponder the moments that fly by fast.

The wind hums low, a life's serenade,
Each rustle a note in nature's brigade.
And I can't help but join the fun,
In the laughter of leaves, my heart's a-run!

Echoes of Growth in the Canopy

Beneath a tree so tall and grand,
The squirrels chatter, oh so bland.
They've started a club, quite absurd,
With acorn snacks, the favored word.

Glimpses of mischief caught in the light,
As pigeons plot from their lofty height.
A coniferous circus, it's clear to see,
Where laughter echoes, wild and free.

Alight Upon Spire and Ridge

When birds wear hats made of twigs and leaves,
And tell tall tales with make-believe.
The raccoons, too, they join the play,
In a dance that brightens the shady bay.

With hidden treasures tucked away,
They giggle and squirm in a playful way.
A whimsical world, all quite absurd,
Where laughter's the language, not a word.

A Journey Through Starlit Pines

As night falls softly with a swipe of stars,
The owls debate their favorite bars.
A party of fireflies start to twirl,
While pine cones dance, giving it a whirl.

The moon peeks down, joins in the fun,
While shadows stretch, not wanting to run.
Together they laugh at the stories they weave,
In a giggly forest, I can hardly believe.

The Magic Within the Trunks

With trees so grand, they prance and sway,
Whispering secrets that lead us astray.
Saplings giggle, in a leafy spree,
Caught in the wind, oh so carefree!

Knotted roots, in a ticklish embrace,
Invite the wanderers to join the race.
Among the bark where laughter springs,
Who knew that trees could have such wings?

Where Time Stands Still in Green

Under the leaves, I sit and wait,
A squirrel races, never late.
The clock's hands twirl, then come to rest,
Nature's silence is truly the best.

Birds gossip loudly about the breeze,
While ants march on, with such expertise.
A dandelion joins the gossiping crowd,
Winking at me, feeling quite proud.

Time forgot here, it's a silly affair,
I argue with shadows but they don't care.
Each tick feels more like a giggle and cheer,
Where moments are sticky like honey, oh dear!

Oh what a joy, life's little charade,
With trees acting wise in their leafy parade.
I hear them chuckle, those trunks with a grin,
As I sip my sweet tea, letting time win.

Reflections on Bark and Bough

A tree once told me a very tall tale,
Of a duck that dreamed it could set sail.
With a quack and a flap, it fell in a pond,
While the willow just sighed and looked quite fond.

The branches above chuckled with glee,
"Why swim," they said, "when you can be free?"
Frogs started dancing, quite out of the blue,
While the sun peeked through, painting skies anew.

A raccoon whispered jokes from the lid of a bin,
"Why did the tree get a sliver? Just kin!"
The stories they share, under old knotted bough,
Are unfurling laughter in each leafy vow.

In this wood, the gossip and fun never cease,
With laughter and joy, my heart finds its peace.
Amongst all the barks and the dueling leaves,
I find humor's echo in all that it weaves.

The Gentle Will of the Woods

In a grove where wisdom turns into jest,
Trees lean in closely, they know what is best.
The oaks drop one-liners with serious flair,
As the pines poke fun, like they just don't care.

"Your bark is worse than your leaf," they declare,
While the birches just giggle, their branches in air.
"Don't leaf us hanging, in the fun, we want in!"
They whisper and chuckle, pulling us into their spin.

A rabbit, bemused, with its ears flopping down,
Claims to be royalty; I can't help but frown.
Yet, all of this nonsense makes perfect sense here,
As laughter erupts, ringing out crystal clear.

So come take a stroll where the breezes are bright,
Join the trees in their antics, let laughter ignite.
For in this green wonder, amid giggles and cheer,
The gentle will of the woods, holds us near.

Inked in Green, the Forgotten Tales

Once upon a time, a leaf had a dream,
To dance in the wind with nothing but steam.
It twirled and it spun, quite the fancy sight,
While the crickets just laughed, "What a quirky flight!"

Old trunks reminisce of a party long past,
With vines laced in laughter, but nothing held fast.
Every rustle, a chuckle, every poke, a jest,
Nature's own comedy, we know it the best.

The mushrooms huddle close, sharing secrets so neat,
About a fox that tripped over his own speedy feet.
A giggle erupts from each roly-poly stack,
As the ferns whisper softly, "Can we have him back?"

In this inked world, memories blend and swirl,
Painted in green, with each flap and twirl.
Forgotten tales of whimsy roam free,
Where laughter sketches life, like a grand jubilee.

The Stillness Within the Thicket

In the thicket, squirrels convene,
Plotting mischief, grass a green screen.
A raccoon dons a mask and a hat,
Hatching schemes to befuddle the cat.

Old owls bicker, hoot with delight,
Sharing secrets deep into the night.
A shy deer giggles at passing cars,
While frogs croon love songs beneath the stars.

The breeze teases, causing a sneeze,
A chorus of chuckles drifts with the leaves.
Every rustle spells a joke untold,
Nature's punchlines sparkling like gold.

In the stillness, laughter takes flight,
With every joke, the world feels right.
Who knew that thickets could be such fun?
Even shadows frolic, dancing in the sun.

A Dance of Sunlight and Shade

Sunlight tiptoes through branches and leaves,
  Casting jokes that the tall tree weaves.
Dancing shadows play hide and seek,
  While the grumpy old pine shakes its peak.

  Squirrels break into a jolly jig,
As a hawk swoops down, doing a wig.
The ferns giggle, ripe with green glee,
  Swaying along like it's a jubilee.

  Caterpillars hold a wild parade,
Mimicking waves, they carry no blade.
Twirling and swirling, oh what a sight,
  In a world where every day's light!

With every gust, the laughter grows,
And the earth hums with the rhythm it knows.
Join the dance, let our joy cascade,
  In this revelry, no worries are laid.

Reveries Under the Conifers

Beneath the conifers, a dream unfurls,
Where pinecones gossip and the wind twirls.
Ducks in bowties swim with such flair,
A raccoon steals snacks from an unsuspecting bear.

Sipping on dew, ants hold their toast,
Toasting the buzz of their busy coast.
A hedgehog winks with a tiny grin,
Living life luxuriously tucked in.

Tree elves giggle behind barky doors,
While squirrels mock-fight, their acorn wars.
With every whisper of leaves above,
The woodland murmurs giggles of love.

In this dreamland, laughter's the king,
With every echo, joy takes wing.
Under conifers, we play and we sway,
Turning each moment into a holiday.

Lost in the Arms of Evergreens

Evergreens cradle the secrets we share,
As chipmunks race by, without a care.
A bear does ballet, quite the rare show,
While rabbits cheer, wearing a bow.

Between juicy berries and sweet honeydew,
The forest conspires to plot something new.
Gnomes tell tales with a twist of the moon,
As frogs jump in rhythm, crooning a tune.

Branches catch laughter, like soft-spun yarn,
As flowers giggle, too shy to warn.
The warmth of the woods makes everything bright,
Who knew the dark could be so light?

In the embrace of the evergreen's grasp,
We tickle the day, with joy we clasp.
So let us roam, with giggles a-boom,
In this forest of whimsy, we find our room.

Secrets Amongst the Sylvan Grove

Whispers of squirrels, plotting their schemes,
Chasing each other, or so it seems.
Under the branches, the rabbits all play,
Giggles and snickers fill up the day.

Old owls on branches, they giggle in glee,
Playing a game of hide-and-seek, see?
The trees stand tall, but they hear all the jokes,
As leaves fall down like confetti from folks.

A hedgehog emerges, wearing a crown,
Strutting his stuff like he owns the town.
The butterflies dance, in color so bright,
Creating a party that lasts through the night.

Secrets are shared where the sunlight streams,
In the heart of the grove, where nothing's as it seems.
With laughter and joy, the woodland's alive,
In this merry place, all creatures can thrive.

Resilience of the Woodland Giants

Tall trees are standing, wrapped up in bark,
Holding their laughter, a quirk and a spark.
Swaying with grace, as wind starts to tease,
Dancing like jesters, oh, if you please!

Acorns are falling, plop, plop, and roll,
Each thud is a joke, a comedic goal.
The forest is chuckling every time one drops,
Like tiny comedians, they get all the props.

Sunlight is filtering, making shadows dance,
The woodland giants love a good prance.
Squirrels are juggling, with flair and with style,
Their acrobatic acts could make any crowd smile.

Resilience abounds among laughter and cheer,
The giants hold up the sky, never fear.
In their wise, rooted ways, they teach us to jest,
That even the mighty can join in the fest.

Echoes of the Green Cathedral

Hush falls the forest, a comedic affair,
As chipmunks do stand-up, without any care.
The echoes of laughter bounce off the trees,
As they share their tall tales with giggles and wheeze.

Under green arches, the critters convene,
Plotting and scheming like royalty keen.
The fawns tell stories of mischievous foes,
While badgers are snickering, no one really knows.

The whispers of mischief float up to the sky,
With each twinkling star a possibility spry.
In the twilight glow, the moon starts to grin,
As owls tell the tales of the shenanigans.

In this grand cathedral of green and of mirth,
Laughter and secrets resonate in the hearth.
With each little creature a story to share,
Under the night sky, they banish all care.

Under the Watchful Boughs

Boughs are like guardians, amusing and wise,
While critters below plot their next little surprise.
Gathered together with snacks all around,
The woodland's a circus; joy does abound.

Frogs croak out jokes that don't always land,
While turtles have puns that are cleverly planned.
A crow caws a punchline just out of view,
Laughter erupts, from the old to the new.

Hares hop along with a comedic flair,
Making the breeze swirl with giggles in air.
They tumble and tumble in playful delight,
As wisdom watches over, snuggly and tight.

So here 'neath the boughs, full of guffaws we sing,
In this wild, wacky world, oh, what joy it brings!
With each friendly laugh, we find our own way,
Under the canopy where silliness plays.

Where the Wild Things Whimper

Beneath the trees, a shy raccoon,
He's got a mask, thinks he's a cartoon.
With banana peels, he wears a crown,
In the twilight, he scampers down.

The owls hoot jokes in hushed delight,
As fireflies dance, lighting the night.
A squirrel's acrobatics bring the cheer,
With his clumsy flips, we all just sneer.

The big bears snore in a silly way,
Dreaming of cupcakes, or so they say.
Dancing hedgehogs steal the pie,
In this jolly world, no one says why.

So here we gather, the forest crew,
Chasing shadows with giggles anew.
Under the stars where laughter looms,
We play all night in nature's rooms.

Poems of the Rooted Realm.

In the land where roots entwine,
The rabbits toast with dandelion wine.
A badger sings of pizza pies,
While all the trees just roll their eyes.

Grasshoppers plan a froggy dance,
Each leap and skip, a wild romance.
Fluttering leaves join in the fun,
As neighbors argue who's won the run.

A wise old oak tells riddles bold,
As mushrooms giggle, secrets unfold.
The ants all march with tiny drums,
Making music, oh what fun it becomes!

So laugh and play, let spirits stream,
In this grounded realm, where life is a dream.
The roots may bind, but joy will swell,
In nature's grip, all laugh and dwell.

Whispers Beneath the Emerald Canopy

Beneath the leaves, a secret band,
With twigs for guitars, they play so grand.
A chipmunk takes the mic with flair,
Singing tunes that fill the air.

The breeze joins in, a singer too,
While crickets chirp, as if on cue.
An old tree grins, deep down it knows,
That laughter among friends always grows.

The raccoon plays on pots and pans,
While frogs form lines, in tall grass they prance.
Each rustle's a cue, the party's alive,
In this leafy throne, all creatures thrive.

So listen close, let joy take flight,
With jokes that swirl like stars in the night.
For under this canopy, life's a jest,
In whispers soft, we are truly blessed.

The Lullaby of Ancient Pines

Among the pines, a fable spins,
With every twig, a tale begins.
An owl with glasses reads the news,
While mice debate their fancy shoes.

The wind carries gossip, soft and sly,
What's that, you say? A turtle's lie!
With shaky voices and shifty eyes,
They laugh so hard, the clovers rise.

Squirrels trade secrets, acorns in hand,
Swapping sweet tales of a nutty band.
A hedgehog giggles, a porcupine grins,
As the sun dips low, the night begins.

So gather 'round, hold each other tight,
In this woodland world, everything's right.
For among the pines, our hearts find tune,
With laughter and love, we'll dance till noon.

Within the Clutch of the Pines

When squirrels plot and scheme overhead,
Their acorns dropped, it's naptime instead.
With smirks, they glance, all mischief and cheer,
While I trip on roots—how'd I get here?

The owls hoot softly, they're critiquing my way,
As branches do jiggles, come join the ballet!
Lichens laugh lightly, they're quite the old crew,
And I'm looking awkward—who's watching? It's you!

The tickling winds tease, they tug at my hat,
Sticky pine sap? Now I'm stuck, imagine that!
Nature's own comedy, it's silly and bright,
I'll close out the day with a giggle or fright.

Underneath the pines, where the laughter is found,
Life's a wild circus; come join in the sound!
With every misstep, another round won,
Here in the woods, joy and folly outrun.

A Haiku for the Heart of the Woods

In trees, whispers play,
A raccoon steals my last snack,
Nature's jesters laugh.

The Exhale of the Exploring Breeze

Chasing the breeze, I wander and roam,
Yet branches confound me; they beckon me home.
As leaves tickle cheeks, I chuckle in glee,
Imagine my grace? It's pure comedy!

Frogs croak their dismay, what a sight I must be,
As I leap like a gazelle—no way could that be!
The brook chuckles too, burbling spells 'round my feet,
I slip on a stone and tumble—quite neat!

Dandelions giggle in meadows so bright,
They tickle my nose in a springtime delight.
With nature as my stage, I put on a show,
Each step, quite the sketch of the wild and the slow.

At dusk, as I'm lost, a firefly's grin,
Winks out from the shadows, 'Come join in the spin!'
With laughter and warmth in this playful maze,
I've danced with the woods in a whimsical phase.

Secrets at the Root's Edge

Down where the roots intertwine and collide,
I find little critters, with humor they hide.
They chuckle in whispers beneath ancient trees,
As I'm trying to listen, they tickle my knees!

The snails, with their swagger, take quite the long stroll,
While rabbits play poker and tease me for being so slow.
In the shade of the ferns, a gossiping throng,
With giggles and chatter, they carry me along.

Each pebble I trip on seems to giggle out loud,
As clouds drift above, somewhat ruffled and proud.
The nature's own jesters share tales 'round the bend,
As I laugh at their antics—each moment, a friend!

So here at the roots, where all secrets unfold,
Life's a wild story, and I'm being told!
With laughter and warmth, I'll forever engage,
In this lively ballet on life's comic stage.

Beneath the Canopy of Whispers

Beneath the leaves so green and wide,
A squirrel debates, should he run or hide?
His stash of acorns, a hefty load,
He's lost his way on a winding road.

A rabbit hops, with style and grace,
Stomping on toes in a frantic race.
With clumsy twirls and leaps so grand,
He steals the show in this woodland band.

Chirping birds crack jokes in tune,
Telling tales of a daring raccoon.
The trees lean closer, giggling in glee,
Nature's laugh, a symphony free.

Under the boughs where shadows play,
Life's a circus in splendid array.
With laughter echoing through the air,
Who knew nature had such flair?

Celestial Songs Amongst Earthly Spires

The stars are winking, a cheeky sight,
As owls recite poems deep in the night.
With every hoot, they test their rhymes,
Creating verses across vast climes.

Dancing fireflies twirl in a line,
Chasing their tails, doing just fine.
They flicker and flitter, no time to waste,
In this nighttime ballet, they're never replaced.

The moon chuckles, casting silvery beams,
While crickets tell tales of impossible dreams.
A froggy croaks, "I need a new hat!"
As laughter erupts from the depths of that.

In this realm where whimsy expands,
Nature's own jesters, with funny commands.
As stars giggle softly, the night rolls on,
In silly harmony, till the break of dawn.

Chasing Shadows in the Thicket

Two chipmunks race through the tangled green,
One yells, "Catch me if you can, Eugene!"
With tiny feet, they zip and zoom,
Creating chaos as they plunder and bloom.

A hedgehog sits, with a frown and sigh,
"My spines are for show, but oh, I'm shy!"
The thorns may protect, but the banter's unkind,
Oh to be bold, if only he'd unwind!

A doe peeks out with a curious eye,
"What's this racket? A ruckus nearby?"
As giggles arise from bushes concealed,
Who knew mischief from nature was so well-revealed?

A raccoon splashes, searching for snacks,
All muddy and sly, he giggles and cracks.
Among the shadows, joy takes its place,
Life's a game with a lively face.

A Pause to Listen to the Owls

In the stillness of night, wise owls convene,
With riddles and puns, keeping it keen.
A game of wits beneath the moon's glow,
Feathers all fluffed, putting on a show.

With beady eyes and a serious stare,
"One puff or two? Tell us, do you dare?"
Their laughs echo softly through hollows and trees,
Tickling the night with a gentle breeze.

Squirrels tune in, with popcorn in hand,
Giggling together, an audience planned.
The owls crack jokes about night's cozy charm,
While crickets cheer on, safe from alarm.

In this woodland stand-up, where shadows unite,
Who needs a spotlight when laughter's so bright?
A pause to listen, the moon's playful jest,
In rib-tickling rhythms, the forest feels blessed.

The Stillness Between Roots

Beneath the branches wide and deep,
Squirrels plot their acorn keep.
They giggle, dart, and chase around,
While sleepy owls make not a sound.

The rabbits dance in leafy skirts,
Complaining 'bout the rise of dirt.
They hop and twirl, a furball spree,
As roots provide the best of glee.

A raccoon plays the serenade,
With moonlight as its soft parade.
The trees just sway, their bowels in knots,
While whispers echo through the spots.

But all is calm, with giggles near,
A rustling leaf sends forth the cheer.
Who knew such fun could spark from gloom?
In nature's lap, there's always room.

Ferns and Forgotten Lullabies

Ferns are dressed in emerald bright,
Whispering tunes in the fading light.
The mossy beds can't hold their laughs,
As crickets sing their silly halves.

A badger dons a sleepy hat,
Claims the forest's his doormat.
He snores in rhythm, soft and light,
His dreams a comedy for the night.

Ghosts of leaves twirl past his paw,
While chipmunks giggle, 'What a flaw!'
They march in lines, a tiny band,
Creating mischief, oh so grand.

Through tangled threads and nightly air,
A song of joy, with just a stir.
Who knew that such a tranquil place,
Could hold such fun, a warm embrace?

Shadows Cast by Gentle Giants

Underneath the towering trees,
Imagination's at its ease.
The shadows stretch, they yawn and sway,
As funny thoughts come out to play.

A fox in shades of copper bright,
Jokes with a beetle, "What a sight!"
They race the sun, a dazzling quest,
In more than just a game of jest.

The trunks stand tall, a lively crowd,
While twigs crack jokes, all nice and loud.
The wind joins in to laugh and swirl,
Creating giggles in a whirl.

These gentle giants, oh so wise,
Hold secrets 'neath their leafy skies.
In every nook the charm persists,
Where shadows come with playful twists.

Serenity Among the Pines

Among the pines, the whispers hum,
A band of lizards, oh so dumb.
They strut about with swagger bold,
While tales of yore just must be told.

The breeze brings laughter, soft and light,
As critters giggle through the night.
They've stashed away their winter gear,
And dance around with nothing near.

A squirrel sneezes, "Achoo! Oh dear!"
While all his friends burst out in cheer.
The pines shake heads in mock surprise,
At all the fun that's shared in guise.

With every rustle, tales unfold,
In laughter wrapped, a joy retold.
Among the pines, the hearts take flight,
In serenity, pure delight.

A Dance Among the Needles

The squirrels held a waltz last night,
With acorns as their shoes, oh what a sight!
They spun and twirled, and then they fell,
Where pine cones rained — oh, can't you tell?

Underneath the branches' sway,
They laughed and played till break of day.
With twigs as swords, and bark for hats,
Who knew that trees invited rats?

The birds joined in with their sweet song,
While dancing leaves played along.
The wind was laughing, a gentle breeze,
As they moved in time with the rustling trees.

So if you wander near and far,
Look for the pine where critters are.
For in the grove, a party unfolds,
With furry guests and tales retold.

The Refuge of Rustling Leaves

Beneath the rustling, leafy dome,
A raccoon claimed it as his home.
With snacks piled high, he feasts alone,
Dreaming of mice on a leafy throne.

A squirrel peeks, oh what a sight!
With nutty dreams that take to flight.
Whispers of secrets in the breeze,
They giggle among the crooked trees.

A party of bugs begins to glow,
As fireflies flicker, putting on a show.
While beetles strut in fancy shoes,
The trees shake their heads, amused by the views.

But all at once, the leaves conspire,
To fall and dance with grace — they tire.
And so the woodland joins the dance,
Where every critter takes a chance!

Underneath the Canopy's Veil

Underneath the leafy shroud,
A worm wriggles, feeling proud.
He claims the title, 'King of Clay,'
While ants march on, come what may.

The grasshoppers play hopscotch bad,
While a ladybug cheers on the lad.
With petals bright, they skip and prance,
In this wild and whimsical dance!

A woodpecker joins with a tap and a hop,
While others chime, 'Don't you stop!'
The dew drops cheer, like tiny drums,
As critters gather, joy to prehum.

So listen close and join the game,
For under this veil, it's never the same.
With laughter shared on high and low,
Nature's stage puts on a show!

Lullabies of the Leafy Veldts

In the fields where the sunflowers sway,
A sleepy hedgehog dozes away.
With the grass beneath a cozy quilt,
He dreams of running — oh, what a thrill!

The bees hum tunes with a buzzing cheer,
While daisies dance without any fear.
Each petal sways, a lovely sight,
Lulling the moon to stay up all night.

The owls hoot softly, 'We're here to play,'
As night wraps the day in a silvery spray.
The stars shine bright, the fireflies gleam,
Whispering secrets of every dream.

So if you wander through fields that glow,
Join the lullabies, enjoy the show.
For nature's heart beats wild and free,
In every leaf, in you, and me!

The Poetry of Needle Against Skim

A pine needle sails down, oh what a sight,
Gliding so smooth, like it owns the night.
Not a care in the world, it dances in air,
While ski poles flail wildly, a comical fare.

The snowmen chuckle, their arms made of sticks,
As skiers tumble and perform funny tricks.
They laugh and they jiggle, their noses all red,
While pine trees stand tall, shaking off their dread.

A sledge full of joy, or maybe a flop,
With every wild laugh, the cold pants won't stop.
In this winter wonder, the humor's just grand,
Where pinecone confetti litters the land.

So let's raise a toast, to the needles and snow,
For laughter and joy, as we all take a bow.
In this frosty ballet, we're all part of the scene,
Finding fun in the antics, where cedar trees gleam.

Frosted Memories of a Silent Night

The moon plays peekaboo, oh, what a game,
As snowflakes prance lightly, dancing the same.
We gather round fires, our marshmallows toast,
Telling tales of the pine, of winter, we boast.

Adventures with squirrels, their acorn heists planned,
While rabbits all giggle, together they stand.
They hop and they skip, oh what a delight,
As we quicken our hearts on this frosty night.

The aire's full of echoes, of laughter and cheer,
With each fumble and tumble, our grins persevere.
In frostbitten fancy, the memories gleam,
As laughter takes flight, like a beautiful dream.

So here's to the shivers, and snowflakes that fall,
To old jokes returning, we share, we enthrall.
In the glow of the darkness, we shine oh so bright,
In frosted memories, we revel in light.

Embracing the Calm Between the Trees

In the quiet we ear, a soft rustling sound,
Where whispers of branches float gently around.
The trees hold their secrets, they're funny, it seems,
With squirrels on stilts, chasing after their dreams.

A pause in the rush, as we sit in the shade,
Imagining wonders, in this leafy parade.
With giggling acorns, falling down in a spree,
Who knew that such joy lay so close to a tree?

We share silly stories, do jokes hit the mark?
From pine cone fashion shows under the dark.
As laughter erupts, we forget all our woes,
In the calm of their branches, a slapstick tableau.

So let's lift our spirits, in this tranquil embrace,
With nature's own humor, we'll all find our place.
For life's little sketches, so easy to see,
In the calm of the woods, happy hearts roam free.

The Language of Twigs and Trunks

Each twig tells a story, each trunk has a tale,
Whispering secrets as winds softly sail.
They chuckle at children who trip on their roots,
And deliberately tickle the toes of grand boots.

The branches are gossipers, flapping away,
Casting love notes in the breeze, night and day.
While shadows do muffle the giggles they share,
The humor of nature—the best kind of flair.

With leaves that are rustling, and laughter they bring,
These trees are the jesters, the laughter they sing.
For every wide grin, each branch knows their worth,
In the midst of this chaos, they anchor our mirth.

So let's join the dance, with each log and each limb,
In this playful theater, we twirl on a whim.
The language of twigs, how they chuckle and hum,
In forests of laughter, where joy's always come.

Reverent Murmurs of the Forest

Squirrels gossip on high, with acorn tales,
They plot and they scheme, like tiny salespales.
Owls blink in surprise, at a crow's silly dance,
While deer watch confused, caught in a trance.

The trees gossip softly, with their leaves all aflutter,
They share juicy secrets, then laugh like a shutter.
A raccoon rolls by, with a mask and a grin,
He's the thief of the forest, where mischief begins.

The shadows all chuckle, with whispers so bright,
As branches poke fun at the moon's silver light.
A breeze teases whispers, from a fern with a flair,
Each rustle's a giggle, as if caught off a dare.

And when nightfall descends, all snug in their beds,
The critters recount tales, with their sleepy little heads.
So if you pass through, listen close in your trek,
For the forest holds laughter, behind every speck.

When Silence Speaks in Wooded Tongues

A fox wearing glasses reads maps in the shade,
He's lost to the woods, but he won't be dismayed.
With a flick of his tail, he waves off a bee,
"You buzzed up my plans! Can't you just let it be?"

Birch trees stand tall, and they grumble aloof,
They gossip about squirrels, a well-rehearsed spoof.
The moss rolls its eyes, with an ancient old voice,
"Why can't we just nap? They've left us no choice!"

A rabbit recites poetry, to no one at all,
While a turtle debates how to jump at a wall.
Each rustle and chatter brings joy to the wood,
If silence was laughter, then all would be good.

So wander through here, where the stillness is thick,
The pines know a joke, and they won't tell you quick.
With every soft creak, a laughter you'll find,
In the whispers of leaves, the woods are so kind.

The Groves' Quiet Ubiquity

In the heart of the grove, where giggles take flight,
A badger bets big on a game of the night.
With paw on his chin, he contemplates fate,
A laugh on the wind says, "You might be too late!"

The ferns shimmy gracefully, swaying with pride,
They know that their edges are the ones to decide.
With snaps and with pops, the green thumbs can flex,
As the squirrels jump in, playing funky reflex.

All around there's a chorus of chortles and cheers,
As trees trade their stories, like old chintzy peers.
An owl hoots a punchline, and it lands with delight,
The night critters chuckle under cloaks of soft light.

So stroll in this space, where joy blooms anew,
A hidden delight, just waiting for you.
For each twig holds a laugh, a secret it shares,
The groves offer wisdom, with whimsical airs.

Whispers of the Woodland Spirits

Beneath every bough, mischief's brewing so sly,
A raccoon throws his hat to the stars in the sky.
With shadows as friends, he plans daring escapades,
Their laughter erupts, like sunflowers in parades.

Whispers flutter through leaves, like tickles in air,
Each breeze has a tale, from here to somewhere.
A chipmunk in stripes, insists he's a knight,
Claiming acorns for quests, by the glow of moonlight.

The spirits chuckle low, as they peek from their home,
While old roots crack jokes, in their earthy dome.
Each ripple in water, a gentle good jest,
Where the world's finest laughter finds its merry rest.

So dive in the woods, with your heart open wide,
For the hum of the forest knows joy cannot hide.
In each twist and each turn, you'll find the divine,
As humor finds life where the sun loves to shine.

www.ingramcontent.com/pod-product-compliance
Lightning Source LLC
Chambersburg PA
CBHW072129070526
44585CB00016B/1587